Art & Activities for Kids

# Paint Adventures!

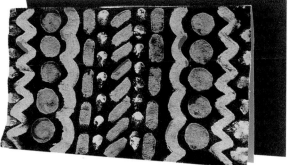

Kathy Savage-Hubbard
Rose C. Speicher

NORTH LIGHT BOOKS

Cincinnati, Ohio

## A Note About Safety

The activities in this book were developed for the enjoyment of kids. We've taken every precaution to ensure their safety and success. Please follow the directions, and note where an adult's help is required. In fact, feel free to work alongside your young artists as often as you can. They will appreciate help in reading and learning new techniques, and will love the chance to talk and show off their creations. Kids thrive on attention and praise, and art adventures are the perfect setting for both.

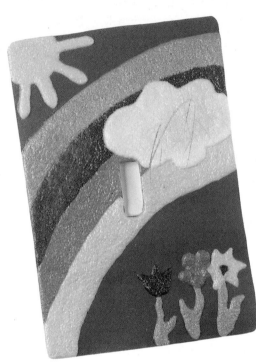

This hardcover edition of *Paint Adventures!* features a "self-jacket" that eliminates the need for a separate dust jacket. It provides sturdy protection for your book while it saves paper, trees and energy.

97  96  95  94  93    5  4  3  2  1

**Library of Congress Cataloging-in-Publication Data**

Savage-Hubbard, Kathy.
 Paint adventures! / Kathy Savage-Hubbard, Rose C. Speicher.
  p.    cm. — (Art & activities for kids)
 Summary: Text and suggested projects using household materials encourage young artists to explore creative ways to use paint.
  ISBN 0-89134-508-6
  1. Art—Technique—Juvenile literature. [1. Painting—Technique.]  I. Speicher, Rose C.  II. Title.  III. Series.
N7430.S23    1993
702'.8—dc20                                    92-45634
                                               CIP
                                               AC

Edited by Julie Wesling Whaley
Design Direction by Clare Finney
Art Direction by Kristi Kane Cullen
Photography by Pamela Monfort
Very special thanks to Theresa Brockman, Eric Deller, Jessica Dolle, Anita Drake, Libby Fellerhoff, Chris Keefe, Alison Wenstrup, Suzanne Whitaker and Rachel Wolf.

*Paint Adventures!* features twenty-six unique painting projects that will fire the imaginations of boys and girls ages six to eleven. Not limited to traditional painting projects, kids have fun making bubble prints (blowing bubbles into paint mixed with soap), marbled paper (capturing the design of paint floating on liquid starch), sand paintings, melted crayon paintings, and two-sided op art (where you see one painting from one direction and a completely different painting from the other direction). It's *easy*, and you need only household materials to get started. Wait until you see how much fun your child has whipping up finger paint with soap powder; mixing paint with salt or glue or both; and making his own puffy paint with flour, salt, water and food colors.

By inviting kids to try new things, *Paint Adventures!* encourages individual creativity. The projects provide clear step-by-step instructions and photographs, and examples of finished works; but each project also is open-ended, so kids may decide what *they* want to paint. In addition, *Paint Adventures!* features a lot of ideas for things to make with the finished paintings. So instead of pitching your prodigy's work of art or letting it languish on the refrigerator door, you can make something useful or decorative out of it, or give it as a gift.

### Getting the Most Out of the Projects

Each project is both fun and educational. In the process of doing the art activities, kids learn about pattern, texture, resist painting, encaus-tic painting, color theory, print-making and much more. But the kids will enjoy learning because the emphasis is on *fun*.

Some projects are easy to do in a short amount of time. Others require more patience and even adult supervision. The symbols explained on page 6 will help you recognize the more challenging activities.

The list of materials at the beginning of each activity is for the featured project only. Suggested alternatives may require different supplies. Feel free to substitute.

Throughout the book you will see "Helpful Hints," which give troubleshooting alternatives. The projects are simple, but something as basic as the thickness of paint sometimes can affect the outcome. So the hints will ensure success and inspire confidence.

### Collecting Supplies

All of the projects can be done with household items or inexpensive, easy-to-find supplies (see page 7 for definitions of art materials you're not already familiar with). Here are some household items you'll want to have on hand: newspapers, paper plates, muffin tins or egg cartons (for holding and mixing paint), margarine tubs (for holding rinse water), drinking straws, cotton swabs, aluminum foil, squeeze bottles (from mustard or dish soap, for example), food colors, plastic bags, shaving cream, white glue, flour, salt, liquid starch, jelly-roll pan, sandpaper and laundry soap powder.

# Be a Good Artist

## Work Habits

Get permission to work at your chosen workspace before you begin. Cover your workspace with newspapers or a vinyl tablecloth.

Wear a smock or big, old shirt to protect your clothes. Cut the long sleeves off of the shirt so you won't drag them through the paint.

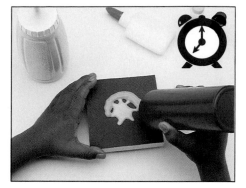

The clock symbol means you must wait to let something dry before going on to the next step. It is important not to rush ahead.

Don't put art materials in your mouth. If you're working with a younger child, don't let her put art materials in her mouth, either.

Follow the directions carefully for each project. When you see this symbol, have an adult help you.

When you see this symbol, look around on the pages of that project for "Helpful Hints." They'll help you get great results.

Most of the things you'll need for each project can be found around the house. Collect your art supplies in a special box.

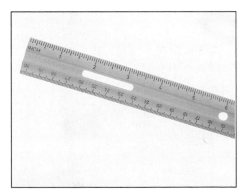

Have a ruler handy. This symbol, ", means inches—12" means 12 inches; cm means centimeters. There are about 2½ centimeters in 1 inch.

Finish by cleaning your workspace and tools. Wash brushes in warm water until the water runs clear, and store them with the bristles pointing up.

## Art Materials

**Tempera paint.** Like poster paint, tempera paint is a water-based paint that is opaque—you can't see through it. Buy it at an art or school supply store already mixed with water, or as a powder that you mix with water (with an adult's help).

**Watercolor paint.** A water-based paint that is transparent—it's thin and watery and you can see through it as you paint with it. It comes in little trays of dry paint that you get wet with a paintbrush and water.

**Acrylic paint.** A water-based plastic paint that's thick and shiny. It comes in a tube or squeeze bottle. You mix it with water to paint with it, but once it's dry, it usually does not wash out.

**Paintbrushes.** There are many kinds of brushes. You may want to buy several, from thin ones to fat ones— even wide house painting brushes. You'll need a sponge brush from the hardware store for the project called "Tempera Batik."

**India ink.** There are lots of kinds and colors of India ink. The best kind to use for tempera batik is black, waterproof India ink. You can buy a small bottle or a large jar at art supply stores.

**Colored sand.** You can find colored sand at craft and hobby stores, or you can get plain, fine sand and color it yourself. One way to color it is to buy colorful chalk and rub it on sandpaper to make powder. Then mix the powder with the sand.

**Acrylic gloss medium.** A type of varnish that's nontoxic. It comes in a spray can or in liquid form that you apply with a brush. Even though it's not toxic, it's still advisable for adults to supervise the use of any spray product.

**Paper.** It's fun to experiment painting on different kinds of paper. The heavier the paper is, the less it will wrinkle and curl as the paint dries. Watercolor paper, from an art supply store, is a very heavy paper with a bumpy texture. If that's too expensive, you can paint on any kind of drawing paper, construction paper, photocopier paper or newsprint. Or ask an adult to bring home used paper from the office and paint on the back.

# Bubble Painting

## Seeing Patterns

Have you ever blown bubbles and tried to catch
them? Try catching colored bubbles on paper!
You will see how the shapes and colors repeat.
That makes a *pattern*. You can use bubble
paintings to color wrapping paper, note cards,
lunch bags, book covers and more.

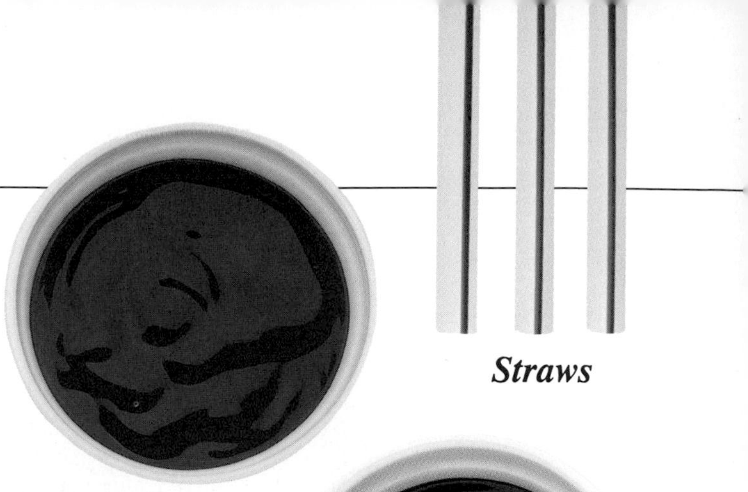

### Materials needed:

*Straws*

*Tempera paint*

*Small bowl*

*Cookie sheet*

*Dish soap*

*Paper*

*Spoon*

This gift wrap and the note card next to it were made with bubble painting.

### *Helpful Hints*

- If you work with a younger child, *make sure* he knows how to blow through a straw. Sucking in the paint mixture could make him sick.
- If you have trouble blowing good bubbles, add one more spoonful of water.
- If your bubbles are a very light color, add one more spoonful of paint.

1 Put 10 spoonfuls of tempera paint, 1 spoonful of dish soap, and 1 spoonful of water in the bowl. Stir. Put a straw in and blow gently.

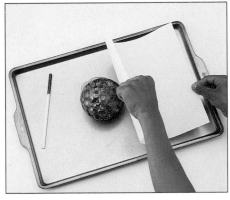

2 When the bubbles rise ½″ to 1″ (2½ cm) above the rim of the bowl, curl a piece of paper and gently touch it to the bubbles.

3 Don't let the paper touch the rim of the bowl. Lift the paper up to see your bubble painting. Let it dry and add another color.

# Melted Crayons

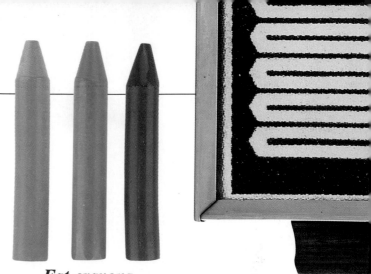

**Fat crayons**

## Encaustic Painting

*Encaustic* painting means painting with wax. Artists used this method in ancient Greece—a long time ago! In this project, you use melted crayons to create paintings rich with color and texture. There are lots of variations to try. You must use heat to melt the crayons, so *ask an adult to help you*. A warming tray works best for safe encaustic painting. If you have permission, you can paint on a cookie sheet, covered with foil, that's been in an oven set at 250°F for ten minutes.

**Materials needed:**

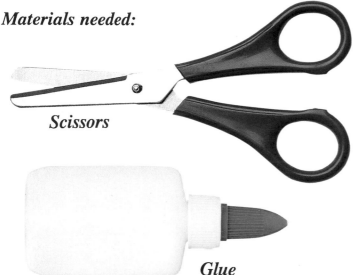

**Scissors**

**Glue**

**Watercolor paints**

**Paintbrush**

***Get Ready.*** Ask an adult to help you with this project. Set the warming tray to "Low." Peel the paper off of fat crayons.

***Draw.*** Place a piece of paper on the warming tray and draw a picture. Draw slowly so the crayon has a chance to melt.

***Comb.*** Get permission to use an old comb or pick to make interesting lines in your painting.

10

**Warming tray**

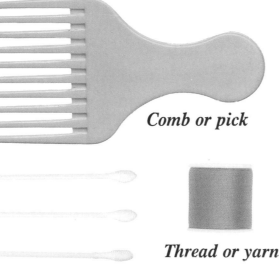

**Comb or pick**

**White paper, foil and cardboard**

**Thread or yarn**

**Cotton swabs**

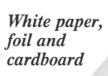

**Stick**

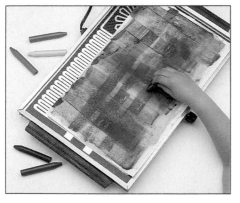

*Fat Lines.* Use the side of a crayon to paint fat lines. *Be careful* not to touch the tray; it gets hot.

*Crumple Foil.* Paint a picture or design. Then crumple foil and press it gently into the melted crayon over and over again to make textures.

*Cut.* When your painting is cool, cut shapes out of it. Hang the shapes from a stick. Or glue them onto another paper to make a collage.

11

# Melted Crayons

***Helpful Hint***
- If at any time you must hold the paper down against the warming tray, wear an oven mitt or hold a crumpled paper towel to protect your fingers from the heat.

The colorful design below was made more interesting by pressing crumpled foil into the colors while they were still warm.

Above is an encaustic turtle, with texture lines drawn with a comb in the melted crayon.

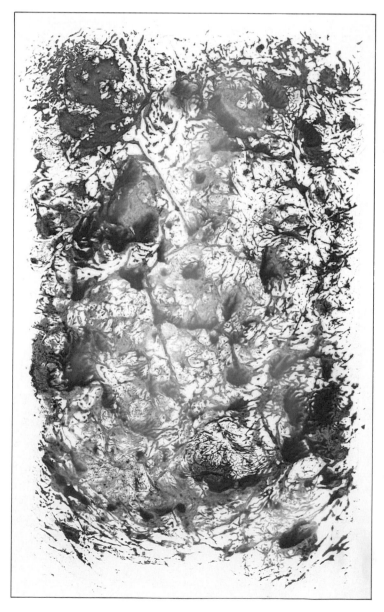

The design to the left is called *plaid*. The wide lines were made by drawing slowly with the sides of the crayons.

Above is a *collage* of shapes cut out of cooled crayon paintings. They look like sea creatures! Blue watercolor paint makes this collage look like an aquarium.

# Melted Crayons

The colorful design at left looks like a flower. Here's how to do it: Crumple foil, then uncrumple it and cover the warming tray with it. Then follow the step called "Pull a Print" on page 15.

Above is an encaustic painting done with crayons melted in muffin tins and painted with cotton swabs. It takes a long time to do a thick painting like this, but the results are beautiful!

The bird mobile to the left is made from shapes cut out of a cooled encaustic painting and hung on a stick with yarn. When you hang them in a window, you can almost see through them!

A finished encaustic painting on foil.

***Paint on Foil.*** Cover the warming tray with foil before you turn it on. Wrap the foil around the handles so it won't slip. Draw on the foil.

***Pull a Print.*** Cover the tray with foil and draw a picture. Lay a piece of paper on top and gently rub with a wadded-up paper towel. Lift the paper.

***Cotton Swabs.*** Put crayon bits into a muffin tin on the warming tray, one color in each cup. Let them melt. Paint with short strokes on heavy cardboard.

# Tempera Batik

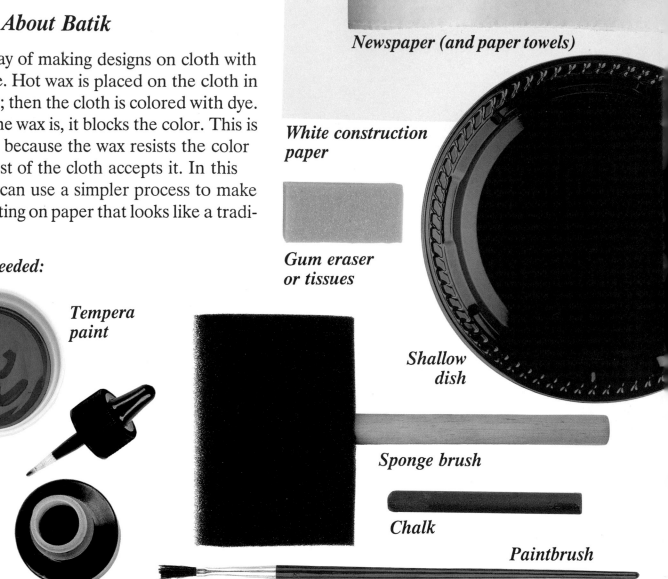

Newspaper (and paper towels)

## Learning About Batik

*Batik* is a way of making designs on cloth with wax and dye. Hot wax is placed on the cloth in some places; then the cloth is colored with dye. Wherever the wax is, it blocks the color. This is called *resist*, because the wax resists the color while the rest of the cloth accepts it. In this project you can use a simpler process to make a resist painting on paper that looks like a traditional batik.

White construction paper

Gum eraser or tissues

## Materials needed:

Tempera paint

Shallow dish

Sponge brush

Waterproof India ink

Chalk

Paintbrush

1 Draw a chalk picture on construction paper. Use thick chalk lines. Make the shapes of your drawing large and simple.

2 Paint inside the chalk lines. Use any color but black. Don't paint over the chalk lines. Leave spaces between the colors.

3 Let the painting dry completely. When it's dry, use a gum eraser or tissues to gently wipe away the chalk lines.

16

A finished tempera batik painting.

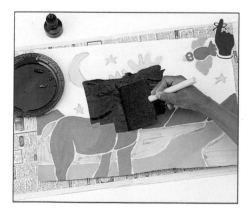

**4** Pour ink into a shallow dish. Use a sponge brush to gently cover the painting with *one* coat of ink. Don't overlap brushstrokes.

**5** Let the ink dry for thirty minutes. Then hold the painting under cool water and gently rub away the ink.

**6** Set your painting on newspaper to dry. Here's how it will look. The ink sticks to the painting in some places, just like a batik!

# Batik Masks and More

Here's a tempera batik that was used as a book cover. Heavy paper pages were tied together with yarn to make a scrapbook.

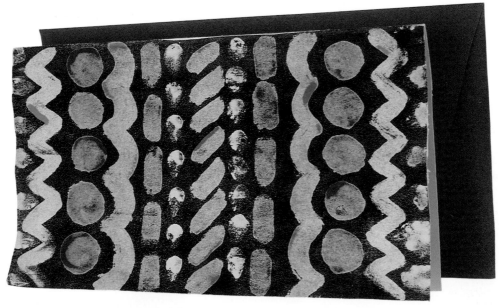

Here's a tempera batik folded in half to make a special card.

18

## Make a Mask

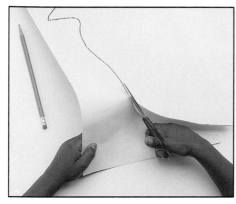

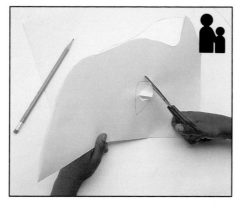

1 Fold a big piece of construction paper in half lengthwise. Draw a curvy, twisting line. Cut along the line; don't cut along the fold.

2 Have an adult help you figure out where the eyes should go. With the paper folded, cut eye holes out of both layers at the same time.

3 Now unfold the mask and batik it, using steps 1 to 6 on pages 16 and 17. Decorate it with feathers, yarn, glitter or sequins if you wish.

When your mask is dry, punch holes on each side and tie yarn at each hole. Tie the yarn behind your head to wear your mask. Don't wear it outside if you can't see well through the eye holes.

### Helpful Hints

- When you wash your paintbrush between colors, dry it with paper towels. It's important for the paint not to be watery.
- *Washable* tempera paint isn't good for this project. It will wash away when you rinse off the ink.
- Only hold your painting under water until the picture appears. Some black will remain. If you soak it too long, you will damage the paper.
- It might help to support your paper on a cookie sheet or board while rinsing.

# Puffy Paint

## Making and Using Textured Paint

Paintings aren't always flat. With common supplies from your kitchen, you can make your own paint that's puffy! Use it to add thick lines to your other paintings. Or use it to decorate boxes, frames, light switch covers and more.

**Mixing bowl and flour, salt and water**

### Materials needed:

**Paintbrush**

**Pencil**

**Food coloring**

**Scissors**

**Glue and acrylic varnish**

**Spoon and small dishes**

**Papers**

**Squeeze bottles**

A finished puffy painting.

1 Mix 1 cup flour, 1 cup water and 1 cup salt. Divide it into several dishes. Add food coloring to make a different color in each dish.

2 If you have several bottles, fill each one with a different color. Then pick up whichever bottle you need and add puffy colors to your painting.

3 If you have only one bottle, squeeze one color in all the places you want that color to be. Then wash the bottle and use it to paint the other colors, one at a time.

# Puffy Stuff

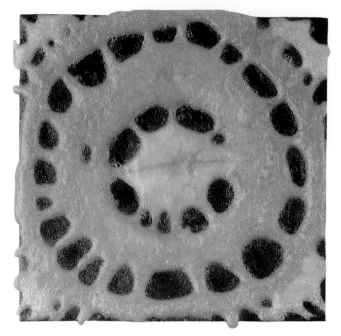

Above is a finished puffy paint box for storing jewelry.

Below is a heart-shaped puffy paint box that would make a great gift filled with candy or little surprises.

## *Cover a Box*

**1** Trace around the bottom of the box on colored paper. Cut out the shape you draw.

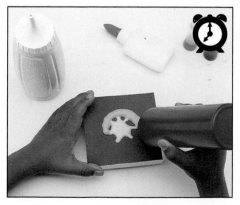

**2** Glue the cut paper to the top of the box. Paint a puffy design following steps 1 to 3 on page 21. Let it dry overnight.

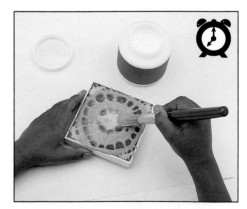

**3** Brush on a coat of acrylic varnish to protect your work and make it shine. Let it dry overnight.

Above is a matboard frame. You can buy matboard at framing stores or art supply or craft stores. Matboard is cut to fit inside of store-bought frames. But if you color a piece with puffy paint, it becomes a beautiful frame all by itself.

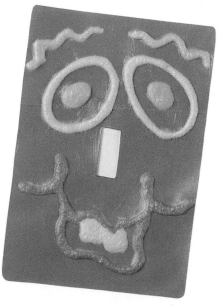

Get permission to make a cover out of heavy paper for your light switch plate. Color it with puffy paint to jazz up your room.

# The Color Wheel

## Color Theory and Experiments

Red, yellow and blue are called *primary* colors. When you mix one primary color with another primary color, you get a *secondary* color. The secondary colors are green, orange, and violet or purple.

In a rainbow, the primary and secondary colors always appear in this order: violet, blue, green, yellow, orange, red. The colors on the color wheel are arranged the same way.

Here's a color wheel with pictures of natural objects that are primary and secondary colors. On the next page are some color experiments to try.

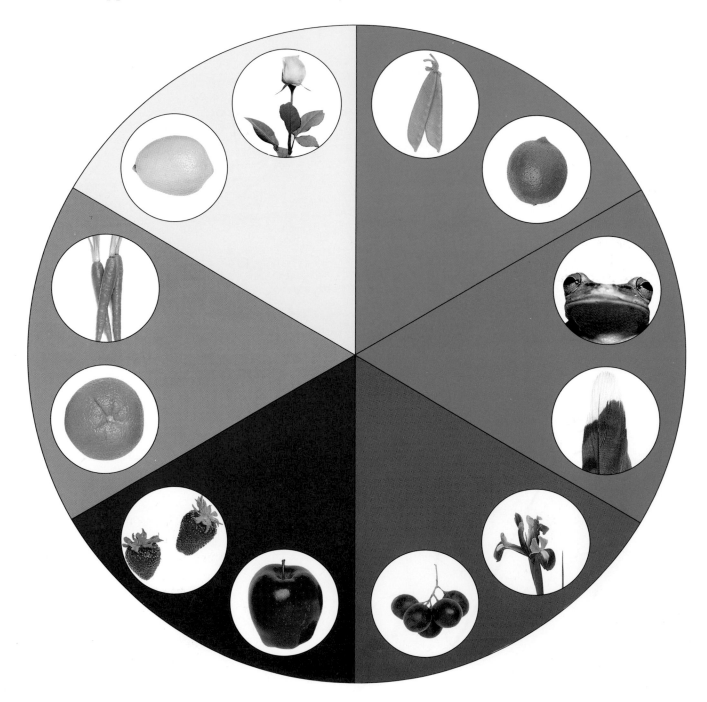

Squirt some foamy shaving cream into a clear plastic bag. Drop food coloring on the sides—one primary color on each side. Seal the bag and squish the shaving cream until the colors mix. Now what color do you see?

Fill a jar with water. Add food coloring one drop at a time and watch the colors slowly blend to make new colors. Try these combinations:

- 1 drop of red + 3 drops of yellow
- 2 to 4 drops of yellow + 2 drops of blue
- 3 to 4 drops of red + 2 drops of blue

*Spinners.* Put a cup on heavy white paper or thin cardboard. Trace around it and cut out the circle. Draw three lines that cross in the center to make six even wedges. Paint every other wedge red. Let it dry. Paint the other wedges either blue or yellow. Push a toothpick through the center. Now spin it like a top. What color do you see? Your eyes will be fooled!

# Color Power

## Mixing Colors

On pages 24 and 25, you can learn about the color wheel. Here is a project to try *using* the color wheel. By mixing the primary colors (red, blue, yellow) you can make the secondary colors (green, orange, violet) and use them in a painting.

**Materials needed:**

*White paper*

*Paintbrushes*

*Paper plates*

*Rinse water*

*Tempera paint: red, blue, yellow*

*Pencil*

**1** Draw a picture that has six of the same shapes, like the diamonds on this snake's back. Paint the first shape red.

**2** On a plate, add yellow paint to red and mix it. The color should be orange. Paint the next shape with the orange paint.

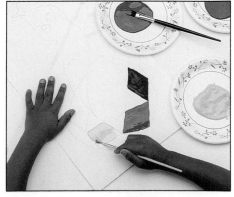

**3** Paint the third shape with the yellow paint.

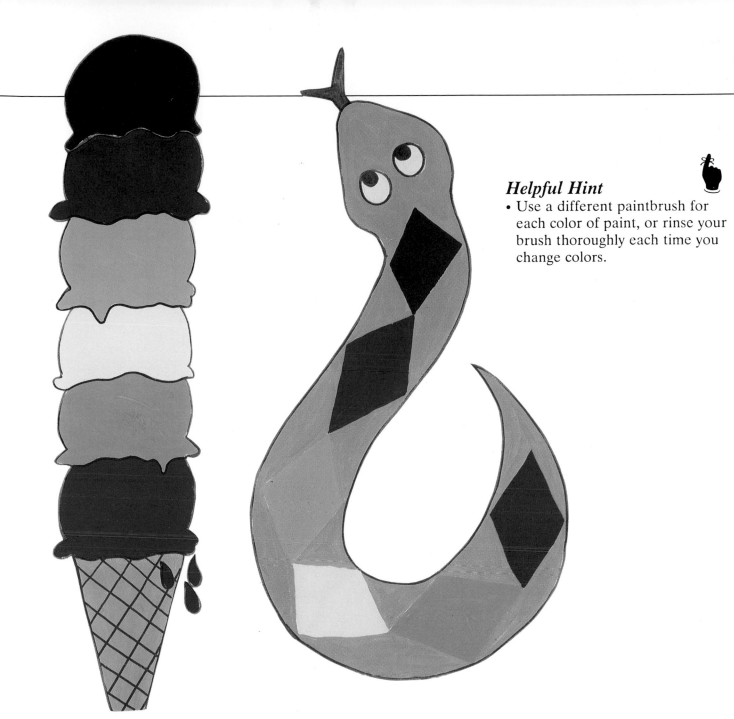

*Helpful Hint*
• Use a different paintbrush for each color of paint, or rinse your brush thoroughly each time you change colors.

4 Add some blue paint to yellow and mix it. The color should be green. Paint the next shape green.

5 Paint the fifth shape with the blue paint.

6 Add some red paint to the blue and mix it to make violet, or purple. Paint the last shape purple. Then paint the rest of the picture.

# Op Art

## Optical Art

In the 1960s, some artists made paintings with geometric shapes that they called *op art*. These paintings were like optical illusions because they tricked people who looked at them. Sometimes the shapes and colors appeared to be moving! Or a viewer might see one painting from one direction, and a different painting from the other direction. (There's an op art project like that on pages 30 and 31.)

Here is a three-dimensional op art project that uses tints. *Tints* are made by adding more or less of a color to white, making it look darker or lighter. You'll see!

### Materials needed:

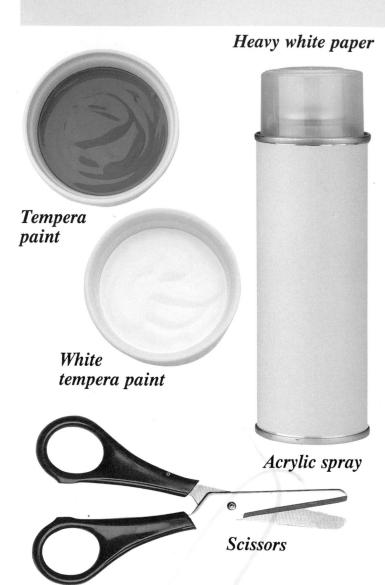

*Heavy white paper*

*Tempera paint*

*White tempera paint*

*Acrylic spray*

*Scissors*

*Paintbrush*

*Pencil*

*Ruler*

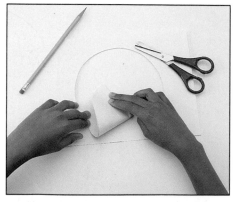

**1** Draw a circle, square, oval or diamond on a piece of white paper. Cut it out. Fold the shape in half and then in half again.

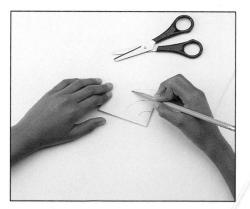

**2** Draw three lines from the side that is one folded edge toward the side that is two folded edges. Don't draw all the way to the end.

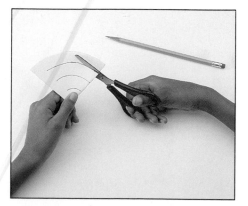

**3** Cut along the lines you drew. Don't cut all the way to the end. Stop where your drawn lines stop. Unfold the shape.

When your hanging is dry, fold half of the center shape toward you and the other half away from you. Then fold the two halves of the ring next to the center the opposite way. Fold the next ring the same way you folded the center. Fold the outside ring the same direction you folded the one next to the center. Use a needle to poke thread or yarn through your op art so you can hang it up.

4 Make a very light tint by mixing a little color with white. Paint the outside ring with it. Let it dry. Paint the other side of that ring.

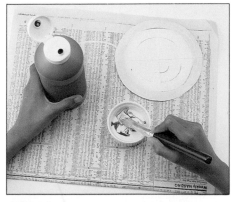

5 Make another, darker tint by adding a bit more color to the first tint. Paint the next ring on both sides with this darker tint.

6 Make the last tint, darker still, and use it to paint the third ring. Paint the middle with the pure color — not mixed with white at all.

# Op Art

If you were to look at your op art unfolded, it would not look like a painting at all. But fold it, and— magic! Walk by it from one direction and see one painting; walk by it from the other direction and see the other painting!

*** Helpful Hint ***

- You may want to use opposite ideas for your paintings such as day and night, winter and summer, or land and sea.

1 Make two paintings, each on a piece of paper 9″ by 12″ (size A4). For true op art, the paintings should be very different.

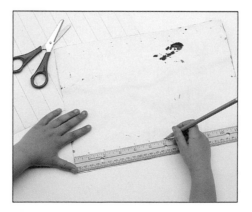

2 When your paintings are dry, turn them over. Make marks 1″ (2½ cm) apart along the top and bottom. Connect the marks with lines to make strips.

3 Number each strip, left to right, from 1 to 12. Do this on both paintings. Cut the strips apart.

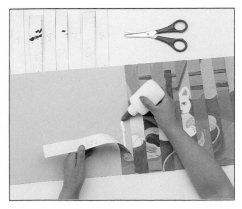

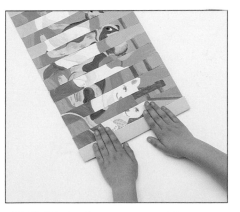

4 Glue the strips onto a piece of heavy paper 9″ (23 cm) by 24″ (61 cm). First do 1 from the first painting, then 1 from the other painting. Then 2 and 2, and so on.

5 Fold the heavy paper like an accordion, using the strips as guidelines for folding. You can make each fold over a table edge to get straight lines.

6 Have an adult help you spray the op art with hairspray or clear acrylic.

# Marbled Paper

## Marbling

*Marbling* is a way of coloring paper to look like a type of stone called marble. Touch paper to paint floating on liquid. When you lift up the paper, you will see beautiful swirls of color.

It's fun to make lots of marbled paper, trying different colors and different swirly patterns. Then, have even more fun *making* things with your marbled paper. See pages 33 to 35 for ideas.

**Cookie sheet**

**Liquid starch**

### Materials needed:

**Paper**

**Pick or pencil**

**Acrylic paint**

**Paintbrushes**

**1** Pour liquid starch on the cookie sheet, about ¼″ (½ cm) deep. Carefully drop watery acrylic paint (2 to 3 teaspoons water to 1 teaspoon paint) onto the starch.

**2** Use the pick or a pencil to make swirls in the colors. Work quickly! The paint will sink into the starch, so you must capture the color while it's still floating.

**3** Curl a piece of paper. Touch the center to the liquid and gently let go of the edges. The paper should sit on the liquid.

Touch a white lunch bag to the swirled paint and make a beautiful gift bag! Marble a piece of paper with the same colors and cut it to make a matching card. This one has a piece of ribbon glued on.

## *Helpful Hints*

- If the paint sinks into the starch right away, you need to mix more water with the paint before dropping it onto the starch.
- It takes a lot of starch to make even a thin layer on the cookie sheet shown here. To save on starch, use a smaller pan and smaller pieces of paper.

4 Gently lift the paper up, starting at one side. The swirls of color will now be on the paper.

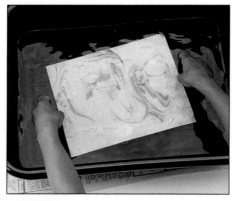

5 Rinse the paper to remove the starchy film. It will take only a few seconds. Don't rinse it longer than that or the paint will come off.

6 Let the marbled paper dry on newspaper. Drip more watery paint onto the starch and you can make another piece of marbled paper.

# Marbled Paper Products

Create a matching desk set by covering a can to make a pencil holder, and a small box to hold paper clips, rubber bands or little treasures.

Make your own book with a marbled paper cover. Cut the cover and all the pages the same size. Make two holes with a hole punch and tie it all together with a ribbon.

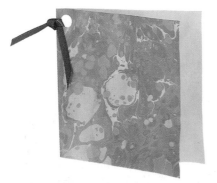

## *Making Combs*

Create your own comb or rake! Make a comb by pushing straight pins through a stick of balsa wood. It is very important that the pins be evenly spaced; these are about ½ cm (less than ¼ inch) apart. Be careful with this sharp tool!

A rake is made of toothpicks taped to heavy cardboard. They are spaced farther apart—about 2 cm (¾ of an inch) between each one.

Experiment dragging these tools up and down and back and forth through the drops of paint floating on the starch. See what designs you can make. Here are a few examples of traditional marbling patterns.

Don't overdo it! For each sheet of marbled paper, only comb or rake through the colors two or three times. Otherwise the colors will run together and look muddy.

Cut a long, thin bookmark and tie a ribbon through a hole punched at the top. Or make a small gift card.

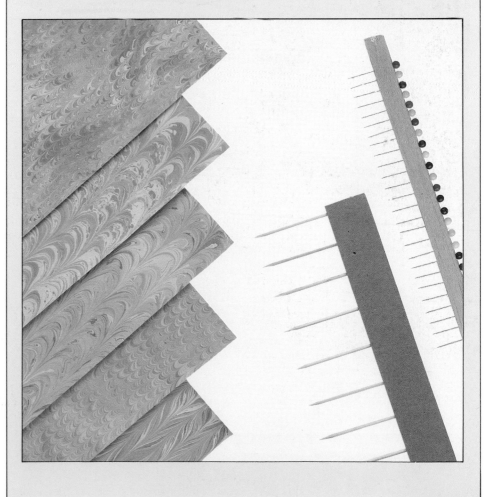

# Scrap Magic

## *Fun Things to Make*

What do you do with your paintings when you're finished painting them? You can make beautiful weavings with two paintings that are the same size (you can cut them to make them the same size if you need to). Or, if you've cut up some of your paintings to make note cards, bookmarks or collages, use the scraps to make paper quilts.

Quilts have been made in America since colonial days. Traditional quilts are sewn with scraps of material. You can make paper quilt squares with scraps of cut paintings. This quilt has pieces of a melted crayon painting, a bubble painting and marbled paper. Cut geometric shapes and arrange them in a pattern on a piece of construction paper. When you make a pattern you like, glue the pieces in place.

This is two salt paintings woven
together. See instructions for making
a salt painting on page 43.

1 Cut slits into one painting.
Don't cut all the way to the
ends.

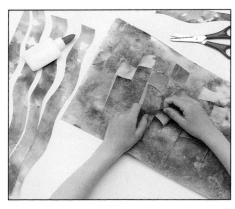

2 Cut the other painting into
straight, wavy, or zigzag strips.
Weave them over and under the
slits in the other painting.

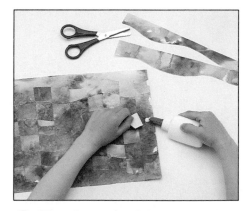

3 Glue the ends of the strips to the
top and bottom edges of the slit
painting.

# Sand Painting

## Navajo Sand Painting

Many years ago the Navajo Indians created paintings in the sand. They colored the sand with powder made from ground-up rocks. The paintings were created for special ceremonies and then destroyed after the ceremony was over. It's easy and fun to make your own sand paintings using sandpaper, glue and colored sand. Imitate traditional Indian symbols or create your own symbols using lines, colors and shapes.

*Colored sand from a craft store*

### Materials needed:

*Feathers and decorations*

*Dish for mixing 1 tablespoon water with 1 tablespoon glue*

1 Draw a design on the sandpaper with a pencil. Choose the colors of sand you want for your design and place them on separate plates.

2 Put the sandpaper on the cookie sheet. Brush the watery glue onto all the sections of your design where the lightest color will be.

3 Use a spoon to sprinkle the lightest color of sand onto the glued sections of your design. Sprinkle on a lot of sand.

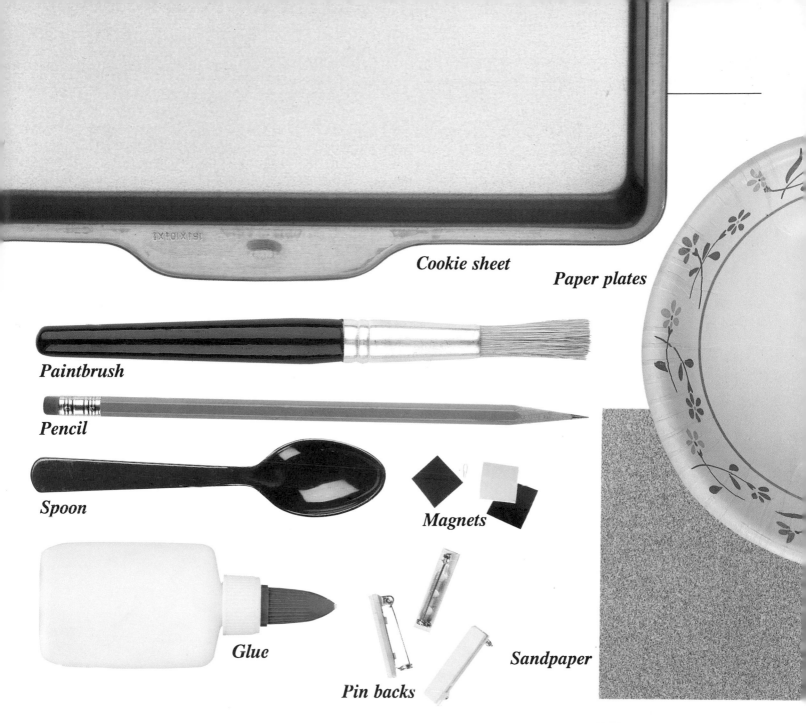

**Cookie sheet**

**Paper plates**

**Paintbrush**

**Pencil**

**Spoon**

**Magnets**

**Glue**

**Pin backs**

**Sandpaper**

4 Turn the sandpaper over and tap it gently. The loose sand will fall back onto the cookie sheet.

5 Set the painting aside to dry for ten minutes. Carefully pour the sand back onto the paper plate.

6 Now do the next color. Brush on glue, sprinkle sand, tap the back, set it aside to dry. Do all the colors this way.

# Sand Painting

Here is an eagle sand painting. The eagle is a traditional Indian symbol. The finished painting was glued to construction paper.

Here is an *abstract* design—it is not meant to look like anything real. It has feathers for decoration! The sandpaper was cut in a circle before painting.

You can cut the sandpaper into little shapes and paint them. Have an adult help you spray them with hairspray or clear acrylic. Then stick magnets or pin backs to the back of them.

Try using colored rice instead of sand. Have an adult help you mix ¼ cup of rubbing alcohol with a few drops of food coloring. Soak the rice for ten minutes, drain it, and set it on waxed paper to dry.

For a natural look, color your own sand by mixing plain, fine sand with cornmeal, ground charcoal, and spices such as cumin, paprika or curry.

# Paint Plus

**Black acrylic and colored tempera paints**

## Creating Textures in Paint

Anyone can paint with paint, but have you ever tried painting with paint plus salt? How about paint plus crayons? Paint plus starch? Glue? Soap? Try all the combinations on the next six pages for some super-special paintings.

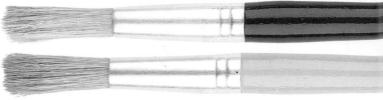

*Paintbrushes*

**Materials needed:**

*Dish*

*Glitter*

*Salt*

*Crayons*

*Paper*

*Glue*

*Watercolor paints and water*

This wet-on-wet painting looks like a flower.

Here's a finished salt painting.

## *Wet on Wet*

## *Salt*

**1** Dip your brush in clean water and wet your whole paper. Then wet one pad of watercolor paint and load the brush. Brush the wet color onto the wet paper.

**2** Try making dots and lines. Watch the color explode! Rinse your brush and add a second color. See how the two colors blend.

Try shaking salt on one of your paintings while it's still wet. Let it dry and then brush off the salt. It will make designs in the paint.

# Paint Plus . . .

. . . Crayons. Use crayons to make rubbings of interesting textures around your house. Then paint over them with watercolors.

. . . Marker. Make a wet-on-wet painting as shown in steps 1 and 2 on page 43. (The colors in this painting look like a sunset.) Draw a scene on top of the painting when it's dry. This black drawing was done with a marker. A black drawing like this is called a *silhouette*.

... Starch and salt. Here's a finished painting done with paint, liquid starch and salt.

**1** Mix ½ cup liquid starch, ⅛ cup water, and ½ cup of salt.

**2** Divide the mixture into several dishes. Add 1 to 2 tablespoons of tempera paint to each dish and stir it up.

**3** Use the mixture to make a bumpy painting. Let the texture and the colors inspire you to paint something from your imagination.

# Paint Plus Glue

Here's a finished paint-plus-glue house.

## Helpful Hints
- It's hard to draw details with glue in a plastic bag, so the larger the shapes are in your picture, the better.
- If you can, keep an old glue bottle, wash it out with warm soapy water, and fill it with the black glue. It will be easier to draw with! You can also buy black glue at some craft stores.

1 Make a pencil drawing on paper. Mix 1 teaspoon of black acrylic paint with 3 teaspoons of white glue. Stir it.

2 Spoon the black glue into a plastic bag. Snip a tiny hole in one corner. Squeeze the glue along your drawing. Let it dry.

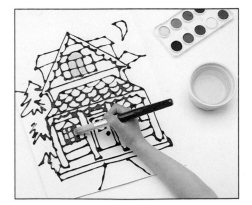

3 Use watercolor paints to color in the shapes you outlined with the black glue.

This alien puppet is painted with tempera paint on lightweight, black cardboard. To make him sparkle, wait for the paint to dry, then draw lines with white glue and sprinkle glitter on the wet glue. He'd look great at night with a flashlight shining on him!

This movie-star puppet has shiny sunglasses, dress and shoes. You can get the same shiny results by mixing tempera paint with a few drops of white glue, then brushing on those areas. Sprinkle on colored glitter while the gluey paint is still wet. The glue in the paint helps the glitter stick to it.

# Paint Plus Soap

Here's a lumpy camel made with paint mixed with soap!

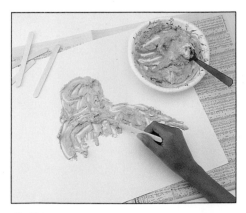

1 Mix 1½ cups of laundry soap flakes with 1 cup of warm water. Beat it with an electric mixer until it's stiff.

2 Divide the soap mixture into several bowls. Add food coloring or paint to each bowl and stir.

3 Use your fingers or craft sticks to spread the thick paint on cardboard or heavy paper.